My Friend Jackson

Written by: Sharon Wasson

Illustrated by: Melinda Wasson

Copyright © 2022 Sharon Wasson
All rights reserved worldwide.

No part of the book may be copied or changed in any format, sold, or used in a way other than what is outlined in this book, under any circumstances, without the prior written permission of the publisher.

Publisher: Inspiring Publishers,
P.O. Box 159, Calwell, ACT Australia 2905
Email: publishaspg@gmail.com
http://www.inspiringpublishers.com

 A catalogue record for this book is available from the National Library of Australia

National Library of Australia The Prepublication Data Service

Author: Sharon Wasson
Title: My Friend Jackson
Genre: Children's Literature
ISBN: 978-1-922792-59-4

For Jackson, remember our differences make us awesome.

We are all born different

none of us the same.

Some of us have bright red hair and wear it with flare.

Some of us have eyes of blue

and jump like
a kangaroo.

Some of us are tall

and some of us are small.

12

We are all born with different skin.

Some of us are wide,

some of us are thin.

My friend Jackson

was born super special!

We have the same nose

but not the same fingers and toes.

Just you watch and see

Jackson can do things, just like me.

He plays in the sand, just like me.

He rides a bike,
just like me.

My friend Jackson is awesome just like me.

www.ingramcontent.com/pod-product-compliance
Lightning Source LLC
Chambersburg PA
CBHW041215240426
43661CB00012B/1054